7. Thomas Blacklock , 1721-1791, Annan

Thomas Blacklock, who was blind from infancy, was something of a phenomenon in his day, being referred to with respect by Samuel Johnson, Edmund Burke and David Hume, although his poems today are not thought to be deeply original. He is perhaps best remembered for his kindly encouragement of other authors, most famously of **Robert Burns**, who decided against emigration to Jamaica upon reading Blacklock's generous appreciation of his *Poems, Chiefly in the Scottish Dialect*.

8. Hugh Clapperton , 1788-1827, Annan

Hugh Clapperton, born at Annan, was the first European to cross the region of Central Africa from the Bight of Benin to the Mediterranean. The journals of his travels testify to the extraordinary bravery and resilience required on these pioneering explorations.

9. Frank Miller, 1854-1944, Annan

Frank Miller was a resident of Annan and devoted himself to the study of the literature of Dumfriesshire: his work on the poets and writers of the area is marked by a scholarly attention to sources and a meticulous investigation of original manuscripts. Along with William Macmath, and **Dr George Neilson,** he was one of those whose collections of Dumfries and Galloway literature laid the foundations of the modern collections at the Ewart Library and Broughton House, Kirkcudbright. He was particularly expert on the Border and Dumfriesshire ballads.

10. Rev C(harles) H(ill) Dick, friend of John Buchan, 1875-1952, Moffat

CH Dick was minister of St Mary's United Free Church at Moffat from 1910-1919, having also briefly been assistant minister at Stranraer St Ninian's in 1904-1905, in the absence of the resident minister. Perhaps surprisingly, given his long residence in Annandale, his celebrated work *Highways and Byways of Galloway and Carrick* shows an intimate knowledge of the west of the region and remains the best introduction to the history and topography of the area. He was also, from his schooldays, a close friend of John Buchan, who himself came to set four novels or stories in Galloway.

11. Sir William Jardine, 1800-1894, Applegarth, Lockerbie

Sir William Jardine, one of the largest landed proprietors in the county of Annandale, was what might be described as the "grand old man" of ornithology and zoology in the area, and was nationally recognised for his achievements and extensive publications on the subject. His books are highly prized for their lavish illustrations.

12. T

Ec

Thomas at Eccle one of original ar social c philosophic of the ...ccuth century. To his contemporaries, he was the "Sage of Chelsea", a great man to be glimpsed by curious visitors to his

house at Cheyne Row, and for whom, in his last illness, Queen Victoria ordered the streets to be covered in straw to deafen the noise of carriages. His long life spanned the period from the early Romantic movement (when he introduced much German thought and writing to Britain) to the High Victorian period, when he became increasingly isolated, extreme and embittered about the prospects of a mechanised society. His well-known style, "Carlylese", a combination of pulpit oratory and Germanicisms, is unmistakable.

PLACES TO VISIT: The "Arched House", Ecclefechan, is open to the public and is run by the National Trust for Scotland. A statue of Carlyle dominates the head of the village of Ecclefechan.

13. Stewart Lewis, 1756-1818, Ecclefechan

Stewart Lewis was born in Ecclefechan and is best remembered for his versions of the ballad *Fair Helen of Kirkconnel* and pastoral *O'er the Moor amang the Heather*. Like **William Nicholson**, he became a pedlar and ultimately depended entirely on selling his songs and begging food. His lyrics express egalitarian sentiments on slavery, poverty, and include some lively Scots verse, particularly his *The Muse in a Passion*.

14. Charles Kirkpatrick Sharpe, 1781-1851, Closeburn, Hoddam

Charles Kirkpatrick Sharpe, man of letters and dilettante antiquarian, was a friend of Sir Walter Scott's and published some important collections of ballads. He also edited some antiquarian literary curiosities and published some etchings, some of which were prized possessions of Scott.

PLACES TO VISIT: A rare collection of Charles Kirkpatrick Sharpe manuscripts and sketches is held at Broughton House, Kirkcudbright.

15. Henry Duncan, 1774-1846, Ruthwell

Henry Duncan, minister of Ruthwell for 47 years, was distinguished in an extraordinary variety of fields: he rescued from obscurity and decay the world-famous Ruthwell cross, the finest survival from Anglo-Saxon Britain and probably one of the finest monuments of early mediaeval Europe; he founded the first Savings Bank on business principles; he engaged in popular education; he founded two newspapers and discovered fossil footprints at Corncockle Muir quarry.

PLACES TO VISIT: The Ruthwell Savings Bank Museum contains a full display on the life and work of Henry Duncan. Ruthwell Church houses the famous Ruthwell Cross. There is a statue to Henry Duncan at Dumfries and an obelisk to his memory at Mount Kedar, Mouswald.

16. Susannah Hawkins, 1787-1868, Burnswark

Susannah Hawkins' verse cannot be classed as literature, but it may well be a specimen - unusual in having survived at all - of a popular class of verse, which must have been much more extensive than we can now know: it was sold as pamphlets from house to house by travelling packmen. In this case, Susannah Hawkins was both author and seller. She was a well-known figure on the roads in Galloway, and travelled as far as central Scotland and northern England.

17. George Neilson, 1858-1923, Horseclose, near Ruthwell

George Neilson, born at the farm of Horseclose in the eastern part of Ruthwell, was a historian of meticulous scholarship, with a particular interest in the Scottish history and poetry of the twelfth to fifteenth centuries. He wrote extensively on the history of Annandale, commenting that local history "after all ceases to be local when, as it scarcely ever fails to do, it illustrates the particular working of general principles".

PLACES TO VISIT: Repentance Tower, near Hoddam, featured in one of Neilson's many articles, may be visited.

18. Robert Burns, 1759-1796, Ellisland and Dumfries

The figure of Robert Burns towers like a colossus over Scottish culture and letters: for any writer since, and, perhaps, for any Scot, whether attracted or repelled by Burns's antithetical qualities, a reaction of some kind has been inevitable. Each generation has reshaped Burns's image to suit its own requirements and preoccupations : the mythological figures of the divinely inspired "ploughman poet" or the drunken debaucher are now being replaced by a more balanced view of Burns's acquaintance with early Scots poetry and Enlightenment thinking. His fame rests largely on the 34 carefully chosen poems of the "Kilmarnock Edition" (1786), but the work he did after moving to Dumfriesshire in 1788 includes his lengthiest and most masterly work, *Tam O' Shanter* and the important work he did to rescue Scottish folk song, both by his own original contributions and re-worked versions of traditional compositions.

PLACES TO VISIT: Ellisland Farm, and Burns's House in Dumfries are both open to the public; many places associated with the Bard, like the Brow Well, are also signposted.

19. JM Barrie, 1860-1937, Dumfries

Although the inspiration of JM Barrie's early successes undoubtedly lay in his childhood – and his mother's childhood – home of Kirriemuir in Angus, and the later stimulus to the composition of *Peter Pan* came from his acquaintance with the Llewelyn Davies boys, his boyhood sojourn at Dumfries deserves mention: at the Academy, he received encouragement for his dramatic talents and interests, and he was later to claim that his days at Dumfries were the happiest of his life.

PLACES TO VISIT: Dumfries Academy, as it was when Barrie attended it, has been replaced by modern buildings. Moat Brae, home of the Anderson family, is still standing.

20. Maria Riddell, 1772-1808, Dumfries

Maria Riddell, wife to Walter Riddell of Woodley Park, near Dumfries, was the most accomplished of all **Burns**'s female acquaintances. She was an authoress in her own right and exchanged verses with the poet. She was notoriously involved in the breach with Burns over what has become known as the "Rape of the Sabines" incident, but showed her humanity in a reconciliation with him before his death, and in her balanced and perceptive appreciation of his personality published a fortnight after his death.

PLACES TO VISIT: Ellisland Farm is open to the public and there is a marked footpath to The Hermitage, Friar's Carse, home of Robert Riddell. Goldielea, once Woodley Park, is now a nursing home

21.   Benjamin Bell, 1749-1806, Dumfries

Benjamin Bell, born of a landed family in Dumfriesshire, was author of one of the best-selling works on surgery of his day; it became the textbook for the Edinburgh school of medicine. His essays on agriculture and political economy were recommended by Adam Smith.

22.   Sir John Richardson, 1787-1865, Dumfries

Sir John Richardson, born in Dumfries, was one of the principal Arctic explorers in the era when the North West passage between the Pacific and Atlantic Oceans and the extremity of the American continent were topics of intense scientific and geographical interest. He made no less than three  expeditions northwards, sometimes under conditions of extreme hardship, but nevertheless managed to collect scientific specimens and to write up learned accounts of the observed phenomena.

23.   RW MacKenna, 1874-1930, Dumfries

RW MacKenna, born at Martyr's Manse, Irving Street, Dumfries, became a doctor and specialist in dermatology. Possessed both of medical expertise and of a deep religious faith, he published during the First World War on aspects of death and suffering, which he came to justify by reference to the workings of providence and purpose. His later historical novels, set in the times of the Covenanters, incorporate much Galloway scenery and characters, in a form reminiscent of Crockett.

24.   William McDowall, 1815-1888, Maxwelltown, Dumfries

William McDowall, born in Maxwelltown, spent most of his life as the editor of the influential and moderately Liberal *Dumfries and Galloway Standard*. His work on the *History of Dumfries*, which went into four editions, remains the sole full-length history of the town.

PLACES TO VISIT: Burns' Statue, erected partly through the industry of William McDowall, stands at the head of Dumfries High Street. There is a memorial plaque to McDowall in the Ewart Library, Dumfries.

25.   Thomas Aird, 1802-1876, Dumfries

Thomas Aird became editor of the *Dumfries and Galloway Herald* from 1835-1863; he published several editions of his poetry, which shows a particular descriptive power when dealing with the natural world, and some plays.

26.   John McDiarmid, 1790-1852, Dumfries

John McDiarmid, one of the founders of the *Scotsman* newspaper, was editor of the *Dumfries Courier* for 36 years and had a marked impact on public opinion and standards of reporting in Dumfriesshire. He also published the *Dumfries Monthly Magazine* to provide a platform for local literary talent, and wrote his *Sketches from Nature*, from articles which had  previously appeared in the *Courier*.

JOHN M·DIARMID.

27.   John Mayne, 1759-1836, Dumfries

John Mayne was born in Dumfries on 26th March 1759, just two months after his greater contemporary, **Robert Burns**. Their careers as poets indeed touched at two points, when two of Mayne's poems, which were early examples of the revival of Scots dialect in poetic diction, inspired compositions on similar themes by Burns. Mayne is best remembered, however, for his poem *The Siller Gun*, describing a shooting competition, or "waponshaw" at Dumfries.

PLACES TO VISIT: The original "Siller Gun" is on display at The Observatory, Dumfries Museum.

28.   John Maxwell Wood, 1868-1925, Dumfries

Maxwell Wood was the editor of the influential literary periodical *The Gallovidian* from 1900-1911 and again at a later period, until just before his death in 1925. He also published on Dumfriesshire and Galloway folklore, smuggling, and on Burns' friendship with the Riddell family.

29.   Allan Cunningham, 1784-1842, Blackwood, Dalswinton, Dumfries

Allan Cunningham, born near Dumfries, who was a prolific author of poetry, collector and creator of folklore, and who was known, because of his biographies of artists, as the "Scottish Vasari", is a significant figure in the early Romantic literature of Scotland. He was acquainted with and admired by Hogg, Southey and Scott and is now remembered for the lyrical beauty of such pieces such as *A Wet Sheet and a Flowing Sea* and *The Lovely Lass of Preston Mill*.

30. Robert Service, 1854-1911, Dumfries

Robert Service, who lived from childhood and worked in Maxwellton, Dumfries, became the most noted naturalist of the area, taking on the mantle of **Sir William Jardine**, and specialising particularly in the subject of bird migration. Although he did not produce a *magnum opus*, his 200 articles on zoology and his regular contributions to local newspapers under the pseudonym "Mabie Moss", constitute a formidable corpus of observation on the changing scene of the natural world on the Solway.

31. William Paterson, 1658-1719, Dumfries

William Paterson, born at Skipmyre, near Dumfries, was the founder of the Bank of England, and the chief mover behind the ill-fated Darien expedition to found a Scots colony in Central America. His writings on trade, including the founding of a Council of Trade, his opposition to paper currency, and his reflections on the Union with England and its commercial advantages, were extremely influential at the time, though his name became largely forgotten.

32. William Beattie, MD, 1793-1875, Dalton

William Beattie, born at Dalton in Annandale, trained in medicine, but was extensively engaged in the composition of lavishly illustrated travel books on Scotland and Switzerland, still well-known for their engravings by Bartlett and Allom. He was also on close terms with the literary men and women of his day, and gave medical treatment free of charge to many in the world of letters, including the poet Thomas Campbell, whose life and works he edited.

33. John Morrison, 1782-1853, Terregles

John Morrison, born near Terregles, in Dumfriesshire, was a minor poet and an artist of some talent, whose friendship with Sir Walter Scott and James Hogg, with Sir Henry Raeburn and Sir Thomas Lawrence, and with Thomas Telford, meant that he had access to the elite literary, artistic and engineering circles of his day.

34. John Gerrond , 1765-1832, Kirkpatrick Durham

John Gerrond, born at Kirkpatrick Durham, was author of a slim volume of poems and prose work, the latter largely a description of his travels in America. Though **MacTaggart** dealt scathingly with his works and personality, and **Harper** also dismisses his verses, few of which, he says, contain "much, if any, poetic talent", Gerrond's reputation has been under reconstruction of late, and his poem, *The Peat Moss*, and others on regional events (*Dumfries Rood Fair*), the pleasures of the chase and of drink, are lively descriptions of rural life.

35. James Currie, 1756-1805, Kirkpatrick Durham

James Currie, first biographer of **Robert Burns**, has been alternately revered and reviled for his role in being the first to fix popular perceptions of the national bard. By the time of the centenary in 1896, he came under heavy criticism for his treatment of the poet's "weaknesses" in the first critical edition of Burns's works, which he edited. Largely thanks to the efforts of RD Thornton, Currie's biographer, a more sympathetic image of Currie has emerged, as a writer under pressure to reconcile editorial standards of accuracy with the need to conciliate Burns's enemies, and to raise subscriptions by a popular sale of the works. Currie was also in his own right a noted medical writer, political thinker and philanthropist.

PLACES TO VISIT: Burns Centre, Dumfries, Burns's House and mausoleum, Dumfries, Ellisland Farm, Dumfries.

36. Joseph Thomson, 1858-1895, Penpont, Thornhill

Joseph Thomson, born at a house built by his father at Penpont, and brought up and educated at Thornhill, became one of the great African explorers of the nineteenth century, ranking with Livingstone and Mungo Park. His expeditions, particularly that through the dangerous territory of the Masai, resulted in the opening up of vast stretches of East Africa to British influence, and in successful trade treaties with the Sudanese kingdoms. His proudest boast, however, was that he never shot an African during an expedition, and never lost one of his own men on his expeditions, except by sickness or accident.

PLACES TO VISIT: Thomson's birthplace at Penpont is marked by a plaque; his bust outside his school at Thornhill still stands.

37. Hugh Steuart Gladstone, 1877-1949, Capenoch, by Thornhill

Hugh Gladstone, who lived at Capenoch, Thornhill, and was prominent in civic life in Dumfriesshire, was the most eminent writer on ornithology in the region: his *Birds of Dumfriesshire* is authoritative, and is now a rare book. He was also an authority on aspects of **Burns**'s life.

38. Rev Dr James King Hewison, 1853-1938, Thornhill

James King Hewison was born at Morton Schoolhouse, the son of Alexander Hewison, a respected parish schoolmaster. By profession a minister, Hewison was an historical scholar of some note, writing particularly on ecclesiastical history, including his classic work on the Covenanters, and work on the Ruthwell and Bewcastle crosses.

PLACES TO VISIT: The monument at Dalgarnock Churchyard erected after a campaign by Hewison, may be seen just south of Thornhill. The Ruthwell Cross, housed in the church at Ruthwell, is open to the public, and is interpreted through the display at the Ruthwell Savings Bank museum, which relates the contribution of the **Rev Henry Duncan** to its rescue.

39. Joseph Laing Waugh, 1868-1928, Thornhill

Joseph Laing Waugh, born in Thornhill and intensely attached to his native village, is remembered for his serio-comic fictional works, written in the vernacular and set in Thornhill, and for his collection of traditions, portrayal of "worthies", and record of dialect in the village.

PLACES TO VISIT: A Memorial tablet to Waugh may be seen at Thornhill.

40. William Wilson and Tom Wilson, 1830-1908; 1864-1930, Sanquhar

William and Tom Wilson, father and son, whose family came to the Sanquhar area in the 1690's to develop lead mines at Wanlockhead, were indefatigable collectors of tradition, history and anecdote related to the burgh of Sanquhar, and have therefore ensured that the town has one of the most documented histories in the region.

PLACES TO VISIT: Sanquhar Castle and Cameron's monument are in the town of Sanquhar. There is a good display of local history at the Sanquhar Town House.

41. Rev Robert Simpson, 1795-1867, Sanquhar

The Rev Robert Simpson DD was pastor of the United Presbyterian Church, Sanquhar, for 47 years. He collected the numerous stories preserved in the oral tradition of the area relating to Covenanting times and embodied them in his tremendously popular *Traditions of the Covenanters*, which went through many editions and was at one time as common in the south of Scotland as the Bible itself.

PLACES TO VISIT: An obelisk to the memory of Robert Simpson was erected outside the North Church, Sanquhar. The monument to commemorate the Sanquhar Declaration, 1680, was set up in 1864 and stands on the main street of Sanquhar.

42. James Hyslop, 1798-1827, Sanquhar, Kirkconnel

James Hyslop, born at the Vennel in the parish of Kirkconnel, and later a cow-herd and shepherd in Muirkirk parish, Ayrshire, was the author of *The Cameronian Dream*, a poem relating to a vision of the famous Covenanting martyrs at Airds Moss. The poem was often reprinted, learnt by heart in the south of Scotland and even achieved much celebrity as far afield as the United States.

PLACES TO VISIT: Richard Cameron's grave at Aird's Moss is marked by a memorial. Hyslop's monument on the Crawick Water can be glimpsed from the front of the parish church in Sanquhar.

43. Alexander Anderson ("Surfaceman"), 1845-1909, Kirkconnel

Alexander Anderson, born at Kirkconnel in Upper Nithsdale, lived much of his life as a worker on the railway there. He attained celebrity when he began publishing poetry under the pseudonym "Surfaceman", particularly with his *A Song of Labour*. It was his vernacular poems, however, which made him a household name in southern Scotland : *Cuddle Doon* became a favourite nursery poem.

PLACES TO VISIT: Kirkconnel Station has a plaque in Anderson's honour, while the red sandstone monument, with bust of Anderson in relief, stands in the corner of Kirkconnel cemetery.

44. Peter Rae, 1671-1748, Kirkconnel, Kirkbride and Dumfries

Peter Rae, from a family of Dumfriesshire tradesmen and small farmers, became minister of Kirkbride in Penpont parish, and later of Kirkconnel; he was a mechanic, mathematician and divine, but most importantly, he began a small printing press while minister at Kirkbride, so that his books were the first to be printed in the south of Scotland, at a time when there were barely half a dozen presses in the country. The *Dumfries Mercury*, likely to have been printed by him, and first appearing probably in 1721, is one of the first newspapers to appear outside Edinburgh.

PLACES TO VISIT: Rae memorial, Kirkconnel churchyard.

45. Robert de Bruce Trotter, 1833-1912, St John's Town of Dalry/Auchencairn/Dalbeattie

Dr Robert de Bruce Trotter was descended from a dynasty of Glenkens doctors, who were also keen collectors of Galloway traditions. Dr Trotter's father, **Robert Trotter**, wrote novels and poetry, and collected Galloway antiquities and curiosities, as did his brothers, **James** and **Alexander**. Robert de Bruce Trotter's two volumes of *Galloway Gossip*, one for Wigtownshire and one for the Stewartry of Kirkcudbright, are perhaps the best exemplification of the family knack for recording the unique flavour of life and language in Galloway.

46. Dr James Trotter, 1842-1899, Auchencairn

James Trotter, one of the three literary sons of a literary father, **Dr Robert Trotter** of Dalry, was a member of the fourth generation of Trotters to write poetry and practise medicine. Trotter is chiefly remembered for his *The Clachan Fair*, and the *Song of Freedom*, which attained particular popularity in America.

PLACES TO VISIT: Trotter's tomb is in Kells churchyard, New Galloway.

47. Joseph Heughan, 1837-1902, Auchencairn

Joseph Heughan was born in Auchencairn, in a house built by his father, and remained there throughout his life, as village blacksmith. He is noted for the density of classical and Biblical allusion in his poetry, together with the use of archaic Galloway words. He wrote a version of the satirical poem *The Gallowa' Herds*.

PLACES TO VISIT: Some fine examples of Heughan's metalwork are to be seen at the Stewartry Museum

48. Dr James Muirhead, DD, 1742-1808, Haugh of Urr, Buittle

James Muirhead originated from an old Galloway family, with an estate in the parish of Buittle. He became minister of Urr, and engaged **Alexander Murray** as his assistant, shortly before he died. He is best remembered for his poem *"Bess the Gawkie"*, which was admired by Burns, but he also engaged in a sharp exchange with the poet, after **Burns** lampooned him in an election ballad. Muirhead's reply was said to have wounded the poet keenly.

49. Robert Kerr, 1811-1848, Haugh of Urr

Robert Kerr (sometimes Ker) was born at Midtown of Spottes and in later life lived at Redcastle Farm, near Haugh of Urr, where he was a ploughman. He attained some celebrity for his sentimental poems, written largely in Scots, *The First Fee* and *The Widow's Ae Coo*. *Maggie o' the Moss* is a long narrative poem, drawing on the tradition of *Tam o' Shanter* for its mixture of humour and the supernatural with moral reflection.

50. James Clerk Maxwell, 1831-1879, Glenlair, Parish of Parton

The name of James Clerk Maxwell, whose family estate was at Glenlair, near the village of Parton in the Stewartry of Kirkcudbright, is perhaps the only one in physics which might be mentioned in the same breath as that of Newton and Einstein. Like Newton, he gave a mathematical account of processes in nature – in Clerk Maxwell's case, a coherent notion of the electro-magnetic field – and revealed the electro-magnetic nature of light itself. His notion of the field, as a mathematically configured system, sensitive in each part to change in any other of its parts, was revolutionary, overcoming the problem of the Newtonian "action at a distance"; and it was the contradictions implicit in the notion of a field which stimulated Einstein's thought, and Maxwell's notion of light as a form of electro-magnetic radiation which enabled Einstein to determine the connection between Energy, Mass, and the speed of light, which is the foundation of the Theory of Relativity and the basis for the development of atomic energy. Clerk Maxwell's contribution to the kinetic theory of gases, which was elaborated by Boltzmann into the foundations of statistical mechanics, became one of the pillars of quantum theory. He was therefore a pivotal figure, in a sense perfecting Newtonian science, and yet providing all the material for the great changes in physics which were to rock its foundations in the twentieth century.

PLACES TO VISIT: Parton churchyard contains a memorial to Clerk Maxwell and his tomb; in Corsock church there is a stained glass window in his memory.

51. John Wilson and Samuel Wilson, 1737-1806; 1784-1863, Crossmichael

John and Samuel Wilson were uncle and nephew from an old family from Burnbrae, a small estate near Clarebrand village. Both had a gift for polemic in verse and Samuel had undoubted poetic talent for a wide variety of forms, but, in the absence of a collected volume of his work, became quickly and undeservedly forgotten.

Cont. page 12

AN ALPHABETICAL INDEX TO THE MAP

97 Agnew, Sir Andrew
25 Aird, Thomas
43 Anderson, Alexander
58 Barbour, John Gordon
98 Barke, James
19 Barrie, J M
32 Beattie, William
21 Bell, Benjamin
7 Blacklock, Thomas
75 Brown, Thomas
18 Burns, Robert
90 Cannon, J F
12 Carlyle, Thomas
8 Clapperton, Hugh
63 Clark-Kennedy, Captain A W M
53 Crockett, Samuel R
29 Cunningham, Allan
35 Currie, James
95 Dalrymple, James, 1st Viscount Stair
73 Denniston, Captain J M
10 Dick, Reverend C H, and Buchan, John
89 Donnan, Jeanie
68 Douglas, Thomas, 5th Earl of Selkirk
15 Duncan, Reverend Henry
83 Fraser, Gordon
34 Gerrond, John
56 Gillespie, Reverend W
37 Gladstone, Hugh S
76 Hannay, Patrick
52 Harper, Malcolm M
16 Hawkins, Susannah
55 Heron, Robert
47 Heughan, Joseph
38 Hewison, J K
42 Hyslop, James
6 Irving, Edward
11 Jardine, Sir William
49 Kerr, Robert
59 Landsborough, Reverend David
88 Latinus Stone
84 Lauderdale, John
13 Lewis, Stewart
57 Lowe, John
64 MacAdam, John Loudon
2 MacDiarmid, Hugh (Grieve, C M)
23 MacKenna, R W
66 Mackenzie, W and
   Mackenzie, Rev William
70 MacTaggart, John
4 Malcolm, Sir John
27 Mayne, John

92 Maxwell, Gavin
50 Maxwell, James Clerk
91 Maxwell, Sir Herbert
78 McCormick, Andrew
87 McCulloch, J R
26 McDiarmid, John
24 McDowall, William
82 McKerlie, P H
80 McNeillie, John
3 Mickle, W J
9 Miller, Frank
69 Montgomerie, Alexander
33 Morrison, John
48 Muirhead, Dr James
79 Murray, Alexander
72 Murray, Thomas
1 Neill, A S
17 Neilson, George
67 Nicholson, John
71 Nicholson, William
31 Paterson, William
93 Patrick, John, 3rd Marquess of Bute
44 Rae, Peter
54 Reid, Professor H M B
22 Richardson, Sir John
20 Riddell, Maria
85 Robinson, Samuel
96 Ross, Sir James Clerk
   and Ross, Sir John
81 Ruskin, John
74 Rutherford, Reverend Samuel
65 Sayers, Dorothy Leigh
30 Service, Robert
14 Sharpe, Charles Kirkpatrick
41 Simpson, Reverend Robert
86 Symson, Andrew
5 Telford, Thomas
36 Thomson, Joseph
99 Todd, William
77 Train, Joseph
62 Trotter, Alexander
46 Trotter, Dr James
61 Trotter, Isabella
60 Trotter, Robert
45 Trotter, Robert de Bruce
94 Vaus, Patrick
39 Waugh, Joseph Laing
51 Wilson, John and Wilson, Samuel
40 Wilson, Tom and Wilson, William
28 Wood, John Maxwell

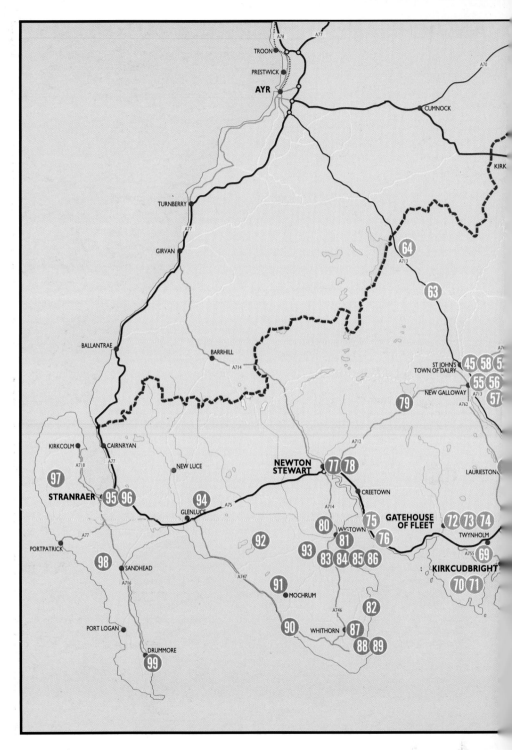

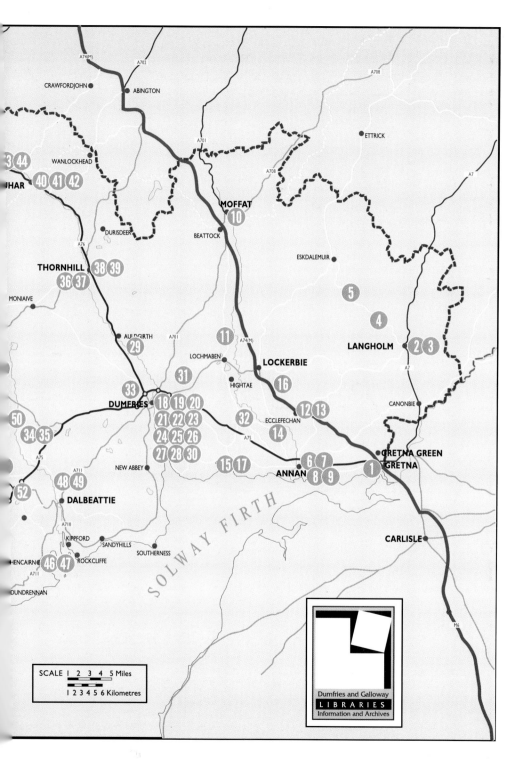

SCALE 1 2 3 4 5 Miles
1 2 3 4 5 6 Kilometres

Dumfries and Galloway
LIBRARIES
Information and Archives

52. Malcolm McLachlan Harper, 1839-1914, Castle Douglas

Malcolm Harper was one of the most significant collectors and promoters of Galloway literature during the nineteenth century; he was responsible for reviving the works of **William Nicholson, Robert Kerr,** republishing minor Galloway poets, and for writing a life of **Crockett**. He also wrote an excellent guide to the historical, etymological, and folkloric material of the province in his *Rambles in Galloway*. The illustrations to this book demonstrate the intimate links between the literary and artistic circles in Galloway at this time, particularly in the Stewartry, where Harper was closely acquainted with the Kirkcudbright school of painters, such as EA Hornel, WS MacGeorge, Blacklock, Henry and Mouncey.

53. Samuel Rutherford Crockett, 1859-1914, Little Duchrae, near Laurieston

Although SR Crockett only lived in Galloway for the first fifteen years of his life, it was to Galloway that Crockett's imagination returned throughout his life and his extraordinarily prolific and varied output, for the inspiration for his best novels and stories. Galloway, particularly in the vicinity of Crockett's birthplace at Little Duchrae, and in the hill country of the Southern Uplands, therefore has the distinction of being one of the three defining landscapes of the "Kailyard" school of Scottish writing, along with **JM Barrie's** "Thrums" and Ian Maclaren's "Drumtochty". "Kailyard" is not, or does not have to be, a term of opprobrium, but defines an extraordinarily popular literary phenomenon, one which was perhaps a necessary outcome of the success of Burns and Scott in defining the Scottish identity and language, and which has certain characteristic features. Crockett's novels, or at least his most successful ones, have in common a generally pre-industrial landscape, a background in which religion plays a strong role, a sentimental love-story and a certain brand of arch humour, of which the two last have aged least well. His best-known novel, *The Raiders*, which sold out within a day of publication, is more than this, however: it is a breathless adventure story in the best tradition of Stevenson and Scott.

PLACES TO VISIT: A memorial to Crockett stands in the village of Laurieston, and his grave is at Balmaghie Church. Classic Crockett country may be visited by walking into the Galloway Hills from Glen Trool.

54. Professor HMB Reid, 1856-1927, Balmaghie Parish

Professor Reid was minister of Balmaghie, the "Kirk above Dee Water", which was **SR Crockett's** parish church and is his place of burial. Reid published extensively on theology, being latterly professor of Divinity at Glasgow University, but his contribution to Galloway literature rests on his sketches of local character, and, particularly, on his documenting his predecessors at Balmaghie, including John MacMillan, one of the founders of the Reformed Presbyterian Church.

PLACES TO VISIT: The Balmaghie church may be visited, and a tablet to John MacMillan may be found in the churchyard.

55. Robert Heron, 1764-1807, New Galloway

Author of a huge and voluminous range of historical and other material, Robert Heron, born in New Galloway in the Glenkens, had an unstable character which prevented his early promise from coming to fruition. He is remembered for composing the first full-length biography of **Burns**, whose contemporary he was and whom he had met, but is blamed for starting a trend in Burns biography which exaggerated the poet's tendency to debauchery. His best work is his first-hand *Observations made in a Journey through the Western Counties of Scotland*, 1793, which gives fascinating insight into conditions in Scotland at the turn of the nineteenth century.

56. Rev William Gillespie, 1776-1825, New Galloway

Rev. William Gillespie, minister of Kells Church, was one of a cluster of poets and writers from the Glenkens of Galloway at the turn of the nineteenth century; he studied at Edinburgh University during the most stimulating period of its Enlightenment, and was in touch with many of the literary men of his day. He was a prolific, though never popular, poet. His principled and unassuming disposition appears to have inspired much respect in his contemporaries.

57. John Lowe, 1750-1798, New Galloway

John Lowe was born at New Galloway, though he later emigrated to Virginia, in the United States. He was known particularly for the affecting ballad *Mary's Dream* and his poetry, though not extensive, was sufficiently known to **Burns** for him to visit the peninsula between the Ken and the Dee, known as "Lowe's arbour", where the ballad was thought to be composed.

58. John Gordon Barbour, 1775-1843, St John's Town of Dalry

John Gordon Barbour came from an old Glenkens family and lived at Bogue House near St John's Town of Dalry, the setting for many of his tales and poems. Like **Denniston** and **Cunningham**, he was a collector of local traditions, and for him, Galloway landscapes were densely populated with legend and figures of history and literature. His *Lights and Shadows of Scottish Character and Scenery* are treasuries of many local legends. His *Queries Connected with Christianity* show a man of intense radical conviction, often painfully at odds with the society of his day.

PLACES TO VISIT: Bruce's Stone at Moss Raploch (NTS) may be visited in the Galloway Forest Park. "Rutherford's Witnesses" stand on a moor above Anwoth village. Both these monuments feature in Barbour's legends.

59. Rev David Landsborough, 1779-1854, St John's Town of Dalry

David Landsborough, descended from the McClambrochs of Stranfasket, and sometime tutor to the family of Lord Glenlee, became a distinguished clergyman and naturalist, particularly known for his study of seaweeds and zoophytes, and his knowledge of the Clyde estuary and of the island of Arran.

60. Robert Trotter, MD, 1798-1875, St. John's Town of Dalry

Robert Trotter was the first in the Trotter dynasty of doctors and writers; he was born at New Galloway and returned to the Glenkens for the latter part of his life, having practised medicine throughout the Stewartry, and elsewhere. His novels, inspired by the Romantic taste for chivalry and the supernatural, are of minor interest, but his collecting of Galloway tales inspired a generation of sons to write on local subjects: **Robert de Bruce Trotter, Alexander and James Trotter.**

61. Isabella Trotter, 1796-1847, New Galloway

Isabella Trotter was the only woman of the Trotter dynasty to write : she was the sister of **Robert Trotter**, and aunt to **Robert de Bruce Trotter, Alexander** and **James Trotter,** all medical men, who celebrated their Galloway birth and inheritance in poetry and prose. She composed a tribute to her father, Robet Trotter, the "Muir-doctor", and wrote some poetry and tales with a local Glenkens setting.

62. Alexander Trotter, 1835-1901, St John's Town of Dalry

Alexander Trotter was a third generation representative of the Galloway family which was unique in combining literary and medical skills: his father, **Dr Robert Trotter of Dalry,** his aunt **Isabella**, and his brother **James** and **Robert Trotter** all wrote, and his grandfather, the "Famous Muir-Doctor" featured in **McTaggart's** *Scottish Gallovidian Encyclopaedia*, had taken **Robert Burns** on a tour of several places of interest in the Glenkens in 1793. Alexander Trotter's own chief literary contribution was through his newspaper articles on Galloway literature and tradition, chiefly published in the *Kirkcudbrightshire Advertiser*, and which were ultimately embodied in his *East Galloway Sketches*: these contributed to preservation of many biographical details and photographs of Galloway writers.

63. Captain Alexander William Maxwell Clark-Kennedy, 1851-1894, Knockgray, by Carsphairn

Captain AWM Clark-Kennedy, born to a family of landed proprietors at Knockgray, near Carsphairn, wrote on ornithology and travel; he also composed poetry, including a poem *Robert the Bruce*, inspired by Walter Scott and describing the places in the hills of Galloway associated with Bruce's military campaigns.

64. John Loudon McAdam, 1756-1836, Waterhead by Carsphairn; Moffat

John Loudon McAdam, born to an old landed family with an estate at Waterhead, was one of the first to devote systematic attention to the method of road-building since the Romans. His contribution came at a point when access by road had a critical part to play in opening up markets for the increasing production of the agricultural and industrial revolutions.

PLACES TO VISIT: McAdam's gravestone exists at Moffat; an informative display on his life and work at Carsphairn heritage centre is within a few miles of his ancestral estate at Waterhead.

65. Dorothy Leigh Sayers, 1893-1957, Kirkcudbright, Gatehouse of Fleet

Dorothy L Sayers was one of the most accomplished writers of detective fiction this century: her polished style, closely reasoned plots and detailed backgrounds established the genre as one worthy of serious literary attention. Her novel, *Five Red Herrings* was set in Kirkcudbright and Gatehouse of Fleet, where houses, personalities and even train times were described with minute and verifiable accuracy.

PLACES TO VISIT: EA Hornel's home, Broughton House, Kirkcudbright (The National Trust for Scotland).

Stewartry Museum, where a Five Red Herrings Trail leaflet is available. Gatehouse station is still visible, and all hotels mentioned are still open to the public.

66. Mr William Mackenzie and Rev William Mackenzie, 1753-1852 and 1789-1854, Kirkcudbright

Both natives of Kirkcudbright, William Mackenzie senior was uncle to the Rev William Mackenzie, master at Kirkcudbright Academy and author of the important *History of Galloway*. The elder Mackenzie was the prolific author of popular moral tracts, aimed at the improvement of young people.

67. John Nicholson, 1778-1866, Kirkcudbright

John Nicholson was among those printers and publishers who, in the history of Dumfries and Galloway, have done much to promote the publication of local literature. His *Historical and Traditional Tales in Prose and Verse, Connected with the South of Scotland* remains a classic selection. He was brother to the famous "Bard of Galloway", William Nicholson.

PLACES TO VISIT: John Nicholson's tomb is in St. Cuthbert's churchyard, Kirkcudbright.

68. Thomas Douglas, 5th Earl of Selkirk, 1771-1820, St. Mary's Isle, Kirkcudbright

Thomas Douglas, seventh son of the Earl of Selkirk and member of a prominent Parliamentary and landowning family, inherited his father's and eldest brother's political concerns and devoted himself to the pressing problem of Highland emigrations. His solution to the crisis was to settle three colonies of Highlanders in western

Canada, and thereby he came to found part of Manitoba and Prince Edward's Island. His schemes had varying success, and his name is still both revered and reviled in the history of Canadian settlement.

PLACES TO VISIT: The Selkirk memorial in the centre of Kirkcudbright is to the 5th Earl's elder brother. St Mary's Isle, the family home, was burnt to the ground in 1940.

69. Alexander Montgomerie, 1555?-1597, Cumstoun, near Kirkcudbright

Alexander Montgomerie was one of the most prominent of the "Castalian" group of poets, formed by the young King James VI of Scotland to experiment with new forms and revive vernacular poetry. Despite his prominence as a poet, little reliable detail has come down to us about his life, but a persistent tradition associates him with the Cumstoun (or Compstoun) estate, near the junction of the Dee and the Tarff outside Kirkcudbright.

PLACES TO VISIT: The Dee at Cumstoun is best viewed from the Tongland Bridge (constructed by Thomas Telford); the ruins of Cumstoun Castle are private.

70. John MacTaggart, 1791-1830, Borgue

Born at Lennox Plunton, near Borgue, John MacTaggart is probably the most Gallovidian of all Galloway authors; his extraordinary *Scottish Gallovidian Encyclopaedia* has been well referred to as a "literary haggis" with its variegated and vigorous sketches of eccentric characters, unusual Galloway words (many of which were thus rescued from oblivion), poems, tales, traditions, antiquities and natural phenomena. The *Encyclopaedia* has borne out its author's confidence that, although the book " will never create much noise, yet it will not be in a hurry forgotten".

PLACES TO VISIT: The Stewartry Museum holds an important collection of material about MacTaggart.

71. William Nicholson, 1783-1854, Borgue

William Nicholson, packman and poet, was known simply as the "Bard of Galloway": he deserves the title not only for his subject matter, or his undoubted devotion to its countryside, but for his use of its living language. His poetry, composed for recitation and singing, includes the *Brownie of Blednoch*, a classic in Scots verse, which has won comparison with *Tam o' Shanter* for its universal treatment of local traditions of the supernatural.

PLACES TO VISIT: The memorial sculpture in Nicholson's memory is located at Borgue school; his tombstone may be seen at Kirkandrews.

72. Thomas Murray, 1792-1872, Gatehouse of Fleet

Thomas Murray, born near Gatehouse of Fleet, made the sole systematic attempt to give a literary identity to Galloway, by tracing its literary traditions across the centuries. Murray lived in an era when regional identity in Scotland was felt and mattered more than it does today, and his own sustained loyalty to Galloway throughout his life made the task of a literary biography of its natives a pressing and appropriate one.

73. Captain James Murray Denniston, 1770-1852, Gatehouse of Fleet, Creetown

James Murray Denniston belonged to a family which had at one time farmed Rusco and remained in the vicinity of Gatehouse of Fleet, having connections with the Murrays of Broughton and Cally. Denniston was a collector of traditions and tales with a local setting, but his best work is his poem *The Battle of Craignilder*, which consists of a vigorous and atmospheric description of the battle between the Black Douglases and the Gordons at Machermore, near what is now Newton Stewart.

PLACES TO VISIT: Cruggleton Castle is among the sites of Denniston's tales which remains open to the public: it may be reached by a cliff-top footpath from Rigg Bay, Garlieston.

74. Samuel Rutherford (Rutherfurd), c1600-1661, Anwoth

Samuel Rutherford became minister of Anwoth in 1628 and remained there until 1637. Though he published scholarly and devotional works throughout his life and later, after leaving Anwoth, attained to much distinction within the Presbyterian church, he is most remembered for his *Letters*, often to parishioners in the neighbourhood of Anwoth and Kirkcudbright: by 1900, there had been over 30 successive editions. His most significant, though least accessible work, is his *Lex, Rex* which set out the mutual rights and relations of king and people, and gained him a reputation as the most considerable constitutional theorist of the Covenanters. His career, ranging from his appointment to a Professorship of Divinity at St Andrew's and his selection as one of the Commissioners to the Westminster Assembly, to citation for treason as he lay dying, demonstrates the extremes of distinction and disfavour to which those at the heart of the turbulent religious politics of the seventeenth century were subject.

PLACES TO VISIT: The ruins of Anwoth Old Kirk, built in Rutherford's day, and Rutherford's Monument, reached by a path from the village, may be visited.

75. Thomas Brown, 1778-1820, Kirkmabreck

Thomas Brown, born at Kirkmabreck, was successor in the Edinburgh University chair of Moral Philosophy to the famous Dugald Stewart, and was the predecessor of John Wilson, alias "Christopher North". He has perhaps been overshadowed by his more flamboyant colleagues, but at the time – which was the summit of the Edinburgh Enlightenment – he was thought to have one of the most acute metaphysical minds in the country.

PLACES TO VISIT: Kirkmabreck's ruined church with obelisk in Brown's memory, stands on the exposed hills above Creetown, with spectacular views of Wigtown Bay and the Solway Firth.

76. Patrick Hannay, ?1594 ; died after 1646, Kirkdale / Sorbie

Patrick Hannay was descended from the house of the Hannays of Sorbie, a branch of which acquired lands at Kirkdale in the Stewartry. He became an accomplished court poet under James VI and I, and his work deals with the characteristic courtly theme of the tortures of the unrequited love for a merciless mistress. It bristles with the elaborate logical and metaphorical conceits expected by a sophisticated and literate audience.

PLACES TO VISIT: Sorbie Tower, Sorbie, ancestral home of the Hannays, is open to the public.

77. Joseph Train, 1779-1852, Newton Stewart and Castle Douglas

Joseph Train, excise officer both at Newton Stewart and Castle Douglas, became one of Sir Walter Scott's most reliable and copious antiquarian researchers, during a correspondence which lasted eighteen years. It was Train's suggestions which prompted Scott to write of Old Mortality, and enabled him to add authentic detail to his story of the Solway Coast, *Guy Mannering*. In his own right, Train wrote an authoritative history of the Isle of Man and of the Buchanite religious sect, based at Crocketford.

PLACES TO VISIT: Plaques to Train's memory exist at the MacMillan Hall, Newton Stewart, and at Castle Douglas. The scenery of *Guy Mannering* and many of its fictitiously named locations, may be found along the coast in the vicinity of Creetown and Barholm.

78. Andrew McCormick, 1867-1956, Newton Stewart

Andrew McCormick, who lived in, practised law in and was Provost of Newton Stewart, wrote the classic and now increasingly rare Galloway book *The Tinkler-Gypsies of Galloway*. He was a noted authority on the travelling people, on Romany language and on "tinkler's cant".

PLACES TO VISIT: Walks taken and described by McCormick can be taken by travelling to Bruce's Stone and Glentrool and following a variety of routes, including a marked climb to the summit of the Merrick.

79. Alexander Murray, 1775-1813, Dunkitterick, parish of Minnigaff

Eighteenth and nineteenth century biographies are full of stories of Scots students who overcome great odds, educational and financial, to become students and prominent men in their field: even in these annals, the story of Alexander Murray, son of a shepherd in the wilds of Minnigaff, has something like legendary status. Murray had a phenomenal talent for languages, speaking and reading more than a dozen, and eventually became Professor of Oriental Philology at Edinburgh: before his early death aged 38, he was in the forefront of those who began to perceive a kinship between European and Indian languages, and thus to found the discipline of comparative philology.

PLACES TO VISIT: Murray's birthplace at Dunkitterick has been preserved by Forest Enterprise, and the monument to his memory is a prominent feature of the Galloway Forest Park.

80. John McNeillie (Ian Niall), 1916 - , North Clutag, near Wigtown

Ian Niall, who first published under his family name, John McNeillie, has celebrated the countryside in more than forty books; he claimed that his *Galloway Childhood* describing his life with his grandparents near Wigtown, was his best work. His work is marked by a profound understanding of the natural world, a crystalline prose style and by the quality of the illustrations accompanying his texts.

81. John Ruskin, 1819-1900, Wigtown

The Wigtownshire connections of one of the most significant art and social critics of the nineteenth century, John Ruskin, are a little known part of his history. Not only was Ruskin related, through his parents, to many of the chief Wigtownshire families (including the **Agnews** of Lochnaw, **the Rosses** of Balsarroch, and the McTaggarts of Ardwell among others) but the person who devoted herself to his care, after the death of his father and during the increasingly serious bouts of "brain fever", was Joan Agnew (Mrs Arthur Severn) who was born in Wigtown. Through her, he gained an affection for the towns of the Solway, which is revealed in his most accessible work, his autobiography *Praeterita*.

PLACES TO VISIT: Wigtown County Buildings now stand on the site of Joan Agnew's home.

82. Peter Handyside McKerlie, 1817-1900, Cruggleton, near Garlieston

McKerlie's *History of the Lands and their Owners in Galloway* has long been a classic of Galloway literature. Though many of his conclusions about early Galloway history have been overturned by more accurate etymological analysis and techniques of archaeological excavation unknown in his time, the value of his recording of family histories and early estate names renders his work still invaluable in the analysis of the shift and continuities of power and land in the hands of the main Galloway families.

PLACES TO VISIT: Cruggleton Castle may be reached by footpath from Garlieston.

83. Gordon Fraser, 1836-1890, Wigtown

Gordon Fraser, druggist, printer, stationer and entrepreneur in Wigtown, is one of the significant minor writers of the area, thanks to whose industry and amused eye for the eccentricities of small town life, we have a well-documented picture of the characters and institutions of Wigtownshire during the nineteenth century.

PLACES TO VISIT: Gordon Fraser is buried at Wigtown Cemetery. The Martyr's Stake, a notorious Wigtown landmark, is signposted east of the town square.

84. John Lauderdale, 1740?–1800?, Kirkinner

John Lauderdale came to live in Kirkinner parish from County Antrim in Ireland in either the 1780's or early 1790's. In 1795, he wrote a reply to **Robert Burns's** Address to the Deil, and in 1796, he published, by subscription, a slim volume of Poems, Chiefly in the Scottish Dialect.

85. Samuel Robinson, 1786-1874, Kirkinner

Samuel Robinson, born at Barglass in the parish of Kirkinner, wrote two autobiographical reminiscences, relating to his boyhood experiences of work aboard a slave ship, and of his early life in Kirkinner parish. Though recollected many years later, Robinson's memories of the Machars of Wigtownshire constitute a valuable eye-witness account of the farming community before the turn of the nineteenth century.

86. Andrew Symson, 1638-1712, Kirkinner

Andrew Symson was Episcopal minister of Kirkinner parish for about 23 years from 1663, the period of the "Killing Times" when the Covenanters were persecuted. His autobiographical comments, scattered throughout his works, enable us to see this period from the point of view of a humane representative of the Episcopalian party. He is remembered for a manuscript A Large Description of Galloway, composed for the Royal Geographer, Sir Robert Sibbald, which contains a unique testimony as to the state of Galloway little more than a hundred years after the Reformation.

87. John Ramsay McCulloch, 1789-1864, Isle of Whithorn, Whithorn and Glasserton

JR McCulloch was born at the Isle of Whithorn, moved to Glasserton Manse before the age of five, after his father's death, and was educated at Whithorn burgh school; ultimately he married Miss Isabella Stewart from Whithorn. It was an unlikely beginning for one of the chief exponents of the emerging science of political economy, but he emerged with James Mill as the most influential exponents of the doctrines of economics developed by Adam Smith and David Ricardo. He began with articles on economics for the fledgling Scotsman newspaper, of which he became one of the first editors; his later Principles of Political Economy was received for many years as a crystalline exposition of the principles of classical economics.

PLACES TO VISIT: Glasserton Manse, which is a private house, may be glimpsed along the road between Port William and the Isle of Whithorn; Glasserton Church still functions as part of a joint charge with the Isle of Whithorn and Whithorn Priory Church; it is open on one Sunday every month.

88. Latinus stone and Miracula Nyniae Episcopi, c. 450 AD and mid-700's AD, Whithorn

It is worth noting that the tradition of literacy in Galloway dates at least to the mid-fifth century, the earliest likely date for the much-discussed "Latinus" stone in Whithorn's Priory Museum. This tradition was flourishing in the mid-700's, when a sophisticated hagiographical poem on the life of St Ninian was composed, possibly at Whithorn. Both works emanated from the Christian church and the later associated pilgrimage centre at Whithorn, which was, according to tradition, founded by Ninian, and later housed his relics.

PLACES TO VISIT: Whithorn Priory Museum houses the Latinus stone; the Priory nave is all that stands of the cathedral complex.

89. Jeanie Donnan, 1864-1942, Whithorn

Jeanie Donnan, who lived in Whithorn for more than half a century, acquired a substantial reputation locally as the "Galloway Poetess", writing odes on local events, and sentimental verses on childhood and nature.

PLACES TO VISIT: A memorial plaque was placed on her house at 76 George Street, Whithorn, by the Editor of the Galloway Gazette.

90. James Fleming Cannon, 1844-1915, Whithorn

James Cannon, a native of Whithorn, where he remained through much of his life, published humorous sketches of life and of the eccentricities of the burgh; he also published numerous poems and short stories, which were never collected, in local newspapers and in *The Gallovidian*, of which he was one of the promoters.

91. Sir Herbert Maxwell, 1845-1937, Monreith

Sir Herbert Maxwell was 7th Baronet of Monreith, descended from a family prominent in Dumfriesshire history, who later settled estates in the Machars of Wigtownshire. He was a prolific writer, author of sixty works in an extraordinary variety of fields: archaeology, philology, arboriculture and horticulture, fishing and shooting, history and biography. He was probably the most gifted scholarly country gentleman in Scotland for the duration of his long life, and for more than a generation no scholarly or public endeavour was complete without his participation.

PLACES TO VISIT: Monreith Gardens are open on a seasonal basis; the House has now been partly converted into holiday accommodation.

92. Gavin Maxwell, 1914-1969, Elrig

Gavin Maxwell, grandson of Sir Herbert Maxwell, was born at the House of Elrig in Mochrum parish, and, through his *Ring of Bright Water*, its sequels, and other books of exploration, became the apostle of the wild to an entire generation. As a record of one man's quest for solitude and for communion with nature, the novel has been ranked with Thoreau's *Walden* or White's *Selborne*, although, as his recent biographer, Douglas Botting , comments "never had the simple life been pursued by so complex a character".

PLACES TO VISIT: An otter sculpture, memorial to Gavin Maxwell, stands at the head of a cliff over Monreith beach. Monreith Gardens, where Mijbil was released into the water of the White Loch of Myrton, are open seasonally to the public.

93. John Patrick, Third Marquess of Bute, 1847-1900, Drumwalt, near Mochrum

The Third Marquess of Bute was born to one of the largest fortunes in Europe, and became the greatest private patron of architecture Britain had ever known. His fascination with mediaevalism led to his celebrated conversion to Catholicism, on which Disraeli based the plot of *Lothair*. His intervention in Wigtownshire, where he worked on his immense translation of the *Breviary*, consisted in the restoration of his own seat at Mochrum, and in extensive archaeological investigations at and around Whithorn, the historical site of St Ninian's "Candida Casa".

PLACES TO VISIT: Whithorn Priory and Museum, Cruggleton Church and St. Ninian's Chapel are all open to the public.

94. Patrick Vaus, ?1530-1597, Barnbarroch, near Whauphill

The correspondence of Patrick Waus, laird of Barnbarroch and an important figure in sixteenth century Scottish court circles, gives a fascinating insight into the life and concerns of a Galloway laird in the period of the Reformation, into the rivalries and frequent brutalities of the relationships between the leading families, and into the epistolary styles and orthography of the time.

95. James Dalrymple, 1st Viscount Stair, 1619-95, Carscreugh, near Glenluce

James Dalrymple, Viscount Stair, acquired the estate of Carscreugh, near Glenluce, and built the tower-house there, whose ruins still stand today. Stair's *Institutions of the Law of Scotland*, largely written at Carscreugh and published in 1681, was quite simply the first systematic exposition of the principles of Scottish private law and the first attempt to found Scotland's positive laws on a rational and philosophical basis. Appearing at the time of the negotiations for a Treaty of Union of Parliaments with England, and indeed, written by one of the chief protagonists of the negotiations, it effectively confirmed the independence of a distinctively Scottish jurisprudence and enabled its survival, even after union with a powerful neighbour possessing a distinctly different legal tradition. The continuing appeal today to Stair in the Scottish Courts, and in the House of Lords, and the daily use of the *Institutions* by practising lawyers, support Stair's claim that "no man did so much, to make the